George Washington

Christi E. Parker, M. A. Ed.

Table of Contents

Who Was George Washington?

George Washington was an important man in American history. He was a hero in the French and Indian War. He led **soldiers** in the American Revolution (rev-uh-LOO-shuhn). Then, Washington became the first president of the new country.

▼ **General George Washington**

Before He Was Famous

George Washington was born in Westmoreland County, Virginia. His father died when he was 11. So, he moved in with his brother, Lawrence. Lawrence owned a large farm in Virginia called Mount Vernon.

At age 16, Washington became a **surveyor** (suhr-VAY-uhr) of land. He helped measure and map new towns in western Virginia.

When Lawrence died, Washington **inherited** (in-HAIR-uh-ted) Mount Vernon. This **plantation** became his home for many years.

◀ **Washington surveying land in Virginia**

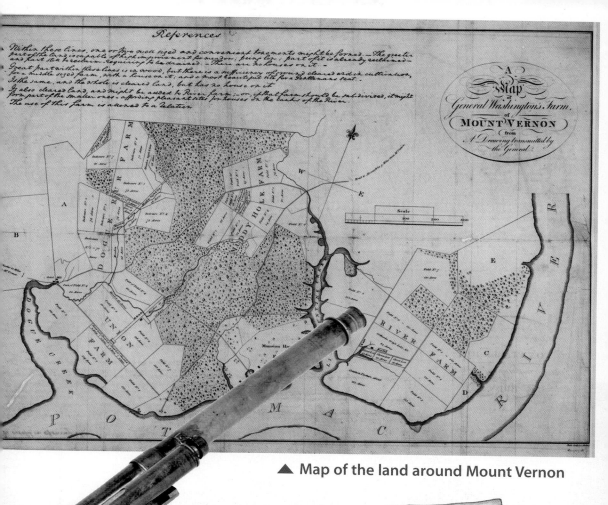

▲ Map of the land around Mount Vernon

▲ Surveying level

When Do We Celebrate?

Washington's birthday is celebrated on February 22. He was actually born on February 11, 1732. Why is there a difference? In 1752, 11 days were added to the calendar. This change helped make the calendar line up with the seasons again.

Joining Forces

In the 1750s, two countries wanted to control the colonies. Both France and Great Britain wanted the new land.

The French were building new **forts**. The forts were used for their army. This made the British **trappers** angry. They needed the land where the forts were built.

France got some American Indian tribes to help them. The French gave guns to the Indians. The Indians used the guns to help France attack the British.

Indians surrounding a British fort ▼

Death of a British general ▲

JOIN, or DIE.

Uniting the Colonies

During this difficult time people thought the **colonists** needed to work together. To help unite them, Benjamin Franklin drew a sketch called "Join or Die." It was the very first American **political cartoon**.

French and Indian War

Virginians wanted their land protected from the French. So, Washington rode to a French fort called Fort Duquesne (dew-CANE). He warned the French to stay away from Virginia.

▲ **Washington going to Fort Duquesne**

Surviving the War

During one battle, Washington had two horses shot from under him. His coat got a bullet hole, too. Washington did not get shot at all!

The French refused to leave. So, Washington and 150 men attacked a group of French soldiers. This started the French and Indian War.

The war lasted from 1754 to 1763. Great Britain won the war. Washington proved to be a skilled fighter.

▲ British troops in red fighting the French troops in blue

Trouble with Britain

In 1759, Washington married Martha Custis. They lived at Mount Vernon. He wanted to farm and live peacefully with his wife and two stepchildren.

The French and Indian War cost Britain a lot of money. Britain wanted to make the colonists pay for the war. The colonists were forced to pay **taxes**.

▲ The wedding of George and Martha Washington

Letters to Martha

When George was away from Martha, he wrote her letters. Before Martha died, she destroyed all but two of the letters. She did not want people to read her private letters.

▲ Mount Vernon, the Washington family home

▲ British tax stamp from 1765

Washington did not think this was right. He went to Philadelphia in 1774. He was part of the First **Continental** (kon-tuh-NEN-tuhl) **Congress**. The Congress decided that the colonies would no longer buy supplies from Britain.

In Charge of a New Army

England kept putting new taxes on the colonies. The colonists decided that they had to go to war. They wanted to be free of English laws. This was the start of the American Revolution.

At the Second Continental Congress, Washington was named **commander** (kuh-MAN-duhr) of the Continental Army.

▼ Washington is named commander in chief.

He knew this was a hard job. The army had a lot of unskilled men. Washington trained them and made them stronger.

His new army went to Boston. There, they set up cannons at night. This surprised the British. Boston was **captured** (CAP-chured) without a fight.

◀ Medal awarded to Washington for the recapture of Boston

His Tattletale Teeth

Washington had false teeth made of ivory. In 1781, he wrote a letter to his dentist. In the letter, he asked for tools to clean his teeth. The British somehow got the letter. This told them where Washington's army was!

Sneaking Up on the British

Washington knew the British had more weapons than he did. Therefore, he had to be very smart to win many battles. Otherwise, the British would overpower his men.

▼ **Washington crossing the Delaware River**

Washington made a sneak attack to capture Trenton, New Jersey. Washington's army crossed the Delaware River on Christmas night. The British did not know they were coming. The colonists landed in Trenton and captured the city. None of Washington's men were hurt in the battle.

Who Else Crossed the River?

James Madison and James Monroe crossed the Delaware River with Washington. They became presidents of the United States, too.

▲ James Madison

▲ James Monroe

Rest for His Men

Washington's men grew tired of fighting. The army rested at Valley Forge, Pennsylvania. They stayed there from December 1777 to June 1778.

There was very little food, and it was a cold winter. Diseases spread in the camp. Many men died. In February, food and other supplies arrived. After that, the army started to get strong.

Washington asked Baron von Steuben to train his soldiers. Von Steuben helped Washington **discipline** the men. Finally, the army was ready to fight the British again.

▲ Baron von Steuben

A Wise Leader

As the commander, Washington could have stayed in a nice warm house at Valley Forge. Instead, he lived in the same cold cabins as his men. This made the men respect him.

▲ Washington at Valley Forge

▲ Valley Forge soldiers' cabin

The End of the War

The last major battle of the war was at Yorktown, Virginia. General Charles Cornwallis led the British. He was waiting for supplies from New York.

▲ Surrender of the British troops

Washington marched to Virginia to catch Cornwallis off guard. Washington asked the French to help. The French set up a **blockade** in the water. Washington blocked the British on land.

Cornwallis was not able to get his supplies. He **surrendered** (suh-REN-duhred) the British armies. The American Revolution was over.

▼ **Victory march through New York**

Washington Becomes President

People knew that Washington was a great leader. So, he was **elected** as the first president of the United States.

Washington believed the country had to have a strong government to be powerful. He asked for help as president. He called his assistants the "**cabinet**."

Short but Sweet

Washington suffered from stage fright. So, he had the shortest **inaugural** (in-OG-yuhr-uhl) **speech** in history.

▲ Washington's inauguration in 178

One time, Washington became upset with Congress. He thought they took too long to make laws. He said he would never go to Congress again. Instead, he would just write letters to them. Presidents still write letters to Congress today.

▼ **Letter from Washington to the House of Representatives**

The President's Message.

ON THE TREATY PAPERS.

CENTINEL-OFFICE, April 7, 1796.

A Gentleman this instant arrived from New-York, has favored us with the following highly interesting and magnanimous Communication of
THE PRESIDENT OF THE UNITED STATES,
to the House of Representatives, on Wednesday the 30th ult.

" GENTLEMEN
" Of the House of Representatives,

"WITH the utmost attention I have considered your resolution of the 24th inst. requesting me to lay before your house, a copy of the instructions to the Minister of the United States, who negotiated the treaty with the King of Great-Britain, together with the correspondence and other documents relative to that treaty, excepting such of the said papers as any existing negociation may render improper to be disclosed.

" In deliberating on this subject, it was impossible for me to lose sight of the principle which some have avowed in its discussion, or to avoid extending my views to the consequences which must flow from the admission of that principle.

" I trust that no part of my conduct has ever indicated a disposition to withhold any information which the Constitution has enjoined upon the President as a duty to give, or which could be required of him by either house of Congress as a right; and with truth I affirm, that it has been, as it will continue to be while I have the honor to preside in the government, my constant endeavour to harmonize with the other branches thereof, so far as the trust delegated to me by the people of the United States, and my sense of the obligation it imposes, to " preserve, protect and defend the Constitution," will permit.

" The nature of foreign negociations requires caution, and their success must often depend on secrecy, and even when brought to a conclusion, a full disclosure of all the measures, demands, or eventual concessions which may have been proposed or contemplated, would be extremely impolitic; for this might have a pernicious influence on future negociations, or produce immediate inconveniences; perhaps danger and mischief, in relation to other powers

government to this moment, my conduct has exemplified that opinion, that the power of making treaties is exclusively vested in the President, by and with the advice of the Senate, provided two thirds of the Senators present concur; and that every treaty so made, and promulgated, thence forward became the law of the land. It is thus that the treaty-making power has been understood by foreign nations; and in all treaties made with them, we have declared; and they have believed, that when ratified by the President, with the advice and consent of the Senate, they became obligatory. In this construction of the constitution, every House of Representatives has heretofore acquiesced; and until the present time, not a doubt or suspicion has appeared to my knowledge, that this construction was not the true one. Nay, they have more than acquiesced; for until now, without controverting the obligation of such treaties, they have made all the requisite provisions for carrying them into effect.

" There is also reason to believe that this construction agrees with the opinions entertained by the State Conventions, when they were deliberating on the constitution; especially by those who objected to it, because there was not required in commercial treaties, the consent of two thirds of the whole Senate, instead of twothirds of the Senators present; and because in treaties respecting territorial and certain other rights and claims, the concurrence of three fourth of the whole number of the members of both houses respectively was not made necessary.

" It is a fact declared by the general convention, and universally understood, that the constitution of the United States was the result of a spirit of amity and mutual concession. And it is well known that under this influence, the smaller States were admitted to an equal representation in Senate, with the larger States

Home at Last

People wanted Washington to be president for a long time. He did not want to be a **dictator** (DIK-tay-tuhr). So, he stepped down after eight years.

Washington moved back to Mount Vernon. He was happy to be home with Martha.

One day, Washington was riding his horse. He became sick with chills and a sore throat. He died that night, on December 14, 1799. He is buried at Mount Vernon.

▼ Washington at Mount Vernon

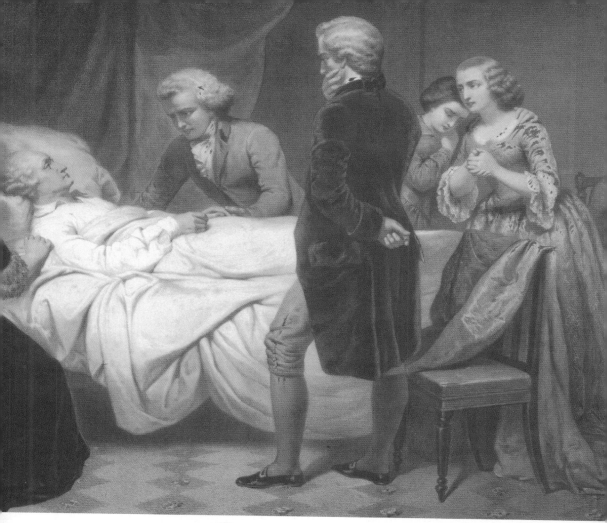

▲ The death of Washington

Choosing a Capital

Washington chose land on the Potomac River for the country's capital. This is where Washington, D.C. is today. Washington never lived there, though. The capital was in Philadelphia when he was president. It took 10 years for the new capital to be built.

George Washington was a hero to many people. He led a young country to victory in the American Revolution. Then, as president, he helped the United States become what it is today.

Glossary

blockade—to block a place from outside contact

cabinet—a group of people the president goes to for advice

captured—caught

colonists—people who settle a new country

commander—the person in charge of an army

Continental Congress—a meeting of the colonists to make laws and decisions

dictator—all-controlling ruler

discipline—to train or teach people to follow directions

elected—voted into office

forts—places where an army stays

inaugural speech—a formal talk given by the president as he takes office

inherited—to receive something after someone has died

plantation—a large farm

political cartoon—a picture that uses symbols and humor to share a point of view

soldiers—people who fight in an army

surrendered—gave up

surveyor—a person who maps out land boundaries and distances

taxes—extra money people pay on goods; this money goes to the government

trappers—people who capture animals for their fur